The Moon Has Got His Pants On and Other Poems

STEVE TURNER

Illustrations by David Mostyn

The Moon Has Got His Pants On and Other Poems

LION
Children's Books

To Lianne and Nathan

Text copyright © 2001 Steve Turner
Illustrations copyright © 2001 David Mostyn
This edition copyright © 2002 Lion Publishing

The moral rights of the author and illustrator
have been asserted

Published by
Lion Publishing plc
Mayfield House, 256 Banbury Road,
Oxford OX2 7DH, England
www.lion-publishing.co.uk
ISBN 0 7459 4584 8

First hardback edition 2001
First paperback edition 2002
3 5 7 9 10 8 6 4 2

A catalogue record for this book is available
from the British Library

Typeset in 12/14 Latin 725 Medium BT
Printed and bound in Great Britain by
Cox & Wyman, Reading

Contents

Introduction

This is my third collection of poetry for children. If you have read The Day I Fell Down the Toilet and Dad, You're Not Funny, you'll know that I like to have a theme to my books; one big idea that helps me to think of all the other little ideas.

The Moon Has Got His Pants On is about the life of one day. The challenge I set myself was to write three poems for every hour of a typical day and night. Each one had to say something about the sorts of things that we might be doing or thinking at that time. Of course, I couldn't write only about the things that I do and think. I had to imagine what other people might be up to. What about the people who have to work while I'm asleep? What about those who have to go to school while I work? And… what about the moon?

Some of these poems should make you think, some will make you laugh, and there are one or two that might make you sad.

I have had fun writing them and hope that you'll enjoy reading them too.

Brand New Day

A brand new day!
Never been used!
Fun for all the family!
Packed with
a guaranteed 24 hours!
Each hour stuffed
with 60 thrill-filled minutes!
Special features include:

* Sunrise!

* Daylight!

* Midday!

* Sunset!

* Darkness!

* Midnight!

Once you have your day
you can do ANYTHING
with it.
There will never be
another day like this!
Collect all 365
for a complete year!

Sleep-overs

Sleep-overs should be banned.
People don't sleep
during sleep-overs.
They eat sweets
during sleep-overs
and make noises
and watch videos
and stay awake.
They should be called
sweetnoisyvideostayawakes
and sweetnoisyvideostayawakes
should be banned
because no one brushes their teeth,
and no one whispers,
and no one shuts their eyes,
and no one sleeps,
and no one gets up in the morning.

Midnight Patrol

The midnight patrol
glides through the night,
on top of the car
blinks a blue light.
Muggers and burglars
slink out of sight
or stand very still
and try to look right.

The midnight patrol
looks left, looks right,
takes care that nothing
slips from its sight,
picks up a flash lamp,
shines down a light,
makes sure that all
stays peaceful tonight.

The midnight patrol
lasts through the night,
doesn't stop searching
until it sees light,
slides into traffic
then out of sight
and doesn't return
until the next night.

Tooth

When a tooth falls out
My mouth feels gappy
But it only shows up
If I get too happy.

Does the House Sleep at Night?

Does the house sleep at night?
Do the carpets all snore?
Do the curtains curl up
in a pile on the floor?

Do the light fittings snooze
as they hang in the air?
Do the cushions relax
in the arms of a chair?

Does the staircase stretch out
as it straightens its back?
Do banisters collapse
with a clickety clack?

Do our beds go to bed
when they see us all doze?
I'm afraid I can't tell
with both my eyes closed.

Nightmare

I'm falling from a window
but I never hit the ground
I try to shout and scream
but my throat won't make a sound
I run with all my strength
but my feet are set in stone
I look for other people
but I'm left all on my own.

I walk along a pathway
but I can't get through the gate
I jump into a taxi
but I'm always much too late
I'm riding on a cycle
but I can't get it to stop
I'm climbing up a mountain
but I never reach the top.

I meet up with my family
but their faces seem to change
I go into my bedroom
but everything is strange
I start to give an answer
but can find no words to say
I wake up in the morning
but the dream won't go away.

Under My Bed

This thing, the one that lies
beneath my bed,
is clever.
It doesn't make a noise.
It never shuffles, rustles or scratches.
Never whispers, screams or moans.
I can't hear its breath.
It lies still.
As still as death.

During the dark hours,
when I call Dad to check it out,
it hears me shout
and slides away. Hides.

Then daylight comes.
It disappears.
The space is bare.
You can peer at where it was
– it's as if it was never there.

How many times
have I seen its shape, its face?
Never.
This thing, this 'it' beneath my bed,
as I have said,
is clever.

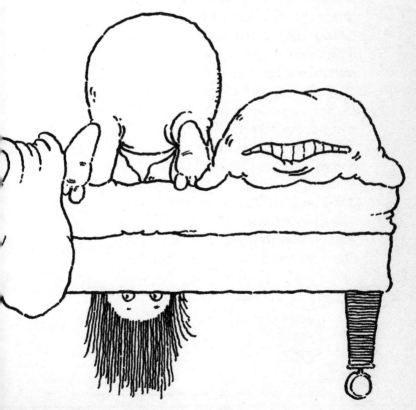

Do I Talk in My Sleep?

Do I talk in my sleep?
If so, what do I say?
Do I shout, do I laugh,
Do I give things away?
Do I sit up in bed
As if back in my class
Giving answers to questions
That no one has asked?

Do I walk in the night?
If so, where do I go?
Do I have my eyes open?
Does it seem that I know?
Do I pack up my bag
Find a clean pair of socks
But never once look at
The time on the clocks?

Do I sleep very still
Like a babe, like a log,
Or wriggle and jiggle
Like a flea-bitten dog?
Do I suck on my thumb?
Do I let out a peep?
I need you to tell me
Because I'm fast asleep.

Waking Up

Waking up, it's 2:52.
Something inside calls, 'You need the loo,'
but you're far too snug to switch on the light
so you lie face down and hope it's all right.

Waking up, it's 3:23.
Something inside says, 'A wee wee wee,'
but outside the bed it's much too cold
so you breathe in deep and you, ah, hold.

Waking up, it's 4:28.
Something inside grunts, 'You just can't wait,'
but you're far too whacked to get up and walk
so you tell that bladder to cut out the talk.

Waking up, it's six on the dot.
Something inside yells, 'It's time to trot,'
but the sun strolls out into the morning sky
so you think to yourself, 'Why bother? Why?'

Waking up, it's 6:59.
Something inside screams, 'It's toilet time!'
so you finally do what you knew you would
and it feels so good, yes, it feels so good.

Is Everyone in Bed Now?

'Not I,' said the baker,
'I'm making new bread.
I stay up all hours
To keep you well fed.'

'Not I,' said the printer
With ink on the drum.
'If *I* slept, there'd be
No *Times*, *Beano* or *Sun*.'

'Not I,' said the doctor
Who's always on call.
'I'm ready for you
Should you slip, crash or fall.'

'Not I,' said the captain
Who trawls the deep sea.
'Your chips would be lonely
If it wasn't for me.'

'Not I,' said the cleaner
Whose truck spins a brush.
'Night streets are empty.
I miss all the rush.'

'Not I,' said the midwife
Who sees children born.
'A baby won't hold on
And wait until dawn.'

'Not I,' said the beggar
Who slumps by a door.
'There's no bed for someone
Who's homeless and poor.'

The Light

A light on
in a window
at 3 a.m.
What could it mean?

Someone dying,
someone crying,
someone up early
for a flight to Spain?
Someone reading,
someone bleeding,
someone who can't sleep
because of the pain?

Someone dozy,
someone nosy,
someone who gazes
through glass at the moon?
Someone rising,
someone revising,
someone whose alarm
has gone off too soon?

Someone lurking,
someone working,
someone telephoned
from the Middle East?
Someone prepared,
someone scared,
someone still eating
a midnight feast?

Someone playing,
someone praying,
someone whose bedbugs
have brought on an itch?
Someone queasy,
someone sneezy,
someone who forgot
to flick off the switch?

Eyelids

Thin curtains of skin,
servants of the eyes,
quick wipers of tears
that only love dries.

Soft shutters of flesh,
whose flickers are nerves,
cleaning technicians
of the eyeball's curves.

Providers of peace
when the world goes mad,
shielders from fear
and anything bad.

Smooth soothers of thought,
protectors from light,
creators of dark
and heralds of night.

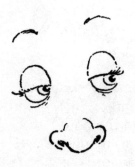

All-Night DJ

I am the soft voice
on the car radio
as the windscreen wipers clack,
the rich soothing tone
over saxophones
on that unknown CD track,
the first word you hear
from the bedside clock
when it makes its morning sound,
a sparkle of hope
for the lonely hearts
when there's no one else around.

I am the sweet noise
in the factory
when the late night shift comes down,
the burble of chat
in the taxicab
that the engine almost drowns,
the unruffled link
before news on the hour
that promises to be right back,
the comforting word
on the FM band
when the sky is deepest black.

Twinkle Twinkle

Twinkle, twinkle, little star.
How I wonder what you are.
To tell the truth, I couldn't care.
I'm down here and you're up there.

What's That Noise?

What's that noise?
It's the sound of healing.
What's that noise?
It's my dead skin peeling.
What's that noise?
It's my nerve ends jumping.
What's that noise?
It's my heart pump pumping.

What's that noise?
It's me blow blow blowing.
What's that noise?
It's my toenails growing.
What's that noise?
It's my tongue lick licking.
What's that noise?
It's my teeth click clicking.

What's that noise?
It's me mum mum mumbling.
What's that noise?
It's my tum tum rumbling.
What's that noise?
It's my eyeballs sweeping.
What's that noise?
It's the sound of sleeping.

The Milkman

It's still dark outside
Silent as night
But here comes that hum
Here comes that light.

The milkman's white float
Glides down the street
Rattle of bottles
Clatter of feet.

A garden gate clicks
Headlight is dimmed
One carton or two
Full-fat or skimmed.

Smoothly he came
Smoothly he goes
The road looks the same
Orange light glows.

Cartons and bottles
Patiently wait
Standing on doorsteps
Lonely and straight.

Adam's Story of Bedtime

It was the middle of the night.
I felt a dig in my ribs,
but thought nothing of it.
Rolled over and dreamed
of vegetation and rivers.

Got up. Washed my face.
Noticed a thin red line
running across my side.
It wasn't there the day before
or the day before that.

I was breathing in and out,
feeling my bones,
when I saw myself
walking towards me.

It was like looking in water
except the hips were different,
the chest, the hair.

The lips parted.
Mine didn't.
'Have you lost something?'
she asked.
'Loneliness,'
I said.

The Morning That Death Was Killed

I woke in a place that was dark
The air was spicy and still
I was bandaged from head to foot
The morning that death was killed.

I rose from a mattress of stone
I folded my clothes on the sill
I heard the door rolling open
The morning that death was killed.

I walked alone in the garden
The birds in the branches trilled
It felt like a new beginning
The morning that death was killed.

Mary, she came there to find me
Peter with wonder was filled
And John came running and jumping
The morning that death was killed.

My friends were lost in amazement
My father, I knew, was thrilled
Things were never the same again
After the morning that death was killed.

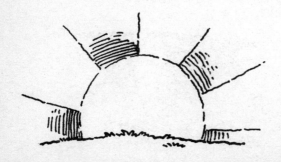

The Morning Lesson

The sun is saying something
As it rises from its bed:
'The light you need to see by
Is right above your head.'

The wind is saying something
As it stirs a storm at sea:
'The things that are important
May be things you cannot see.'

The rain is saying something
As it splashes on the screen:
'I can take your life away
Or make you fresh and clean.'

The tree is saying something
As it stretches to the sky:
'Your roots will hold and feed you
When everything goes dry.'

Dawn Chorus

If I was a bird
I'd wake at six in the morning,
rush into the street
and start singing
at the top of my voice.

My neighbours,
if they too were birds,
would peer through their curtains,
then run downstairs
singing, singing, singing.

We would not all
be singing the same song.
We would be singing
at each other.
We would be singing
to prove who was the loudest,
and who was the prettiest,
and who could sing
the longest song.

We'd be singing, singing, singing,
heads thrown back,
chests thrust out,
throats open wide.
The noise would fill the street.
The noise would sail into the sky.

And somewhere, someone,
who for some reason
was not a bird
would notice
and would say,
'Isn't that lovely!
Can you hear it?
Isn't that lovely!'

The Early Worm

The early bird catches the worm –
She tugs at her juicy fat prize.
The early worm hangs from her beak
As the early bird takes to the skies.

The early worm looks to the ground.
Then up to the early bird's jaw.
He feels a little bit queasy.
He's never been this high before.

The early bird gets to her nest
And drags all her babies from bed.
'See what I've brought back for breakfast
To make sure you children are fed.'

The babies say, 'Oh no, not worm!
We had worm for dinner and tea.
Can't you bring something that's different
Like snailburger, maggot or flea?'

The worm was chopped into pieces
And spread over slices of bread.
Oh, how he wished he'd stayed home
All cosy and tucked up in bed.

It's best not to get up too soon;
That's my advice to young worms.
The early ones end up in birds
As this little story confirms.

Face

Every morning I wash my face.
Mum says to do so is right.
But tell me this: how does a face
Get dirty during the night?

Seven O'Clock News

This is the seven o'clock news
I can't get out of bed
I can't peel back my eyelids
or lift my sleepy head.

I hear the buzzer buzzing
I feel the sun's warm rays
But I'm in another world
I'm lying in a daze.

This is the seven-twenty news
I've rolled onto my side
My brain has started working
My eyes are open wide.

I'm making plans to exit
But need to give it time
One hand has left the duvet
One foot begins to climb.

This is the seven-thirty news
My socks have run away
Someone should have washed my shirt
To stop it turning grey.

My knickers have gone missing
No toothpaste has been bought
If I'm late for school again
It's someone else's fault.

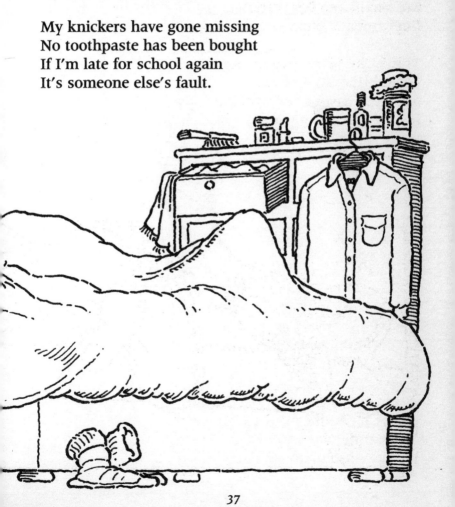

The Mirror

Whenever I look in the mirror
I find that it's me who is there,
Wearing identical clothing
And staring straight into my stare.

I've tried creeping up without warning
And peeking from outside the frame.
But whatever I look like that day
Looks back – it's exactly the same.

I think, can I trick my reflection
And glimpse someone famous or rich?
A model or maybe a film star,
I really don't mind what or which.

Yet it's me who gets in the picture,
Always me in the glass gazing out;
Sleepy, untidy or grumpy.
But me. Absolutely. No doubt.

Breakfast Reading

There are too many words in a novel;
I only have time for the jackets;
but I read everything that is printed
on the backs of cereal packets.

There I learned about soluble fibres
and the dangers of choking on fruit;
that Cheerios contain rice and barley;
that the Coco Pops monkey is cute.

I may not know much about Goosebumps
or the person whose gables were green,
but Kellogg's, I can tell you for certain,
was appointed by HM The Queen.

I don't know what happened to Ratty
or if Alice returned from the hole,
but the thiamin found in Rice Krispies?
It's 0.4 milligrams per bowl.

Who's Stuck in the Bathroom?

Who's stuck in the bathroom?
Who's causing a queue?
Who's squeezed all the toothpaste?
  You.

Who's moved all the brushes?
Who's nicked the shampoo?
Who's clogged up the plughole?
  You.

Who's hogging the mirror?
Who's still on the loo?
Who's used the hot water?
  You.

Who's shouting and knocking?
Who can't have a wee?
Who's fed up with waiting?
  Me.

Packed Lunch

Sandwich, crisps,
biscuit and drink.
Bring your own food.
School dinners stink.

Where Mum Drives Me

My mum's a good driver.

She drives me batty
She drives me to the edge
She drives me bonkers
She drives me off my head.

She drives me loopy
She drives me till I jump
She drives me bananas
She drives me off my chump.

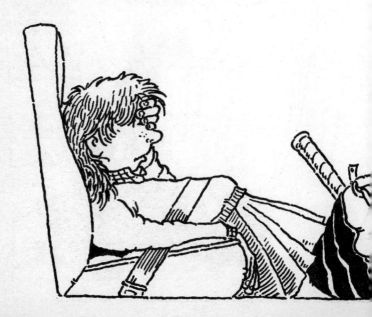

She drives me potty
She drives me to the end
She drives me gaga
She drives me round the bend.

She drives me crazy
She drives me up the wall
She drives me scatty
And she drives me to school.

Assembly

We assemble.
That's why it's called
assembly.
We sit cross-legged.
The area of the bottom
multiplied by the number of pupils
is greater than the area
of the hall floor.
We squiggle, we squeeze,
we squash, we squabble.
Jamie is asked to stay behind.
Behind is another word for bottom.
Miss walks on the stage.
So does Miss, Miss, Sir,
Miss, Sir, Miss, Miss and
Miss.

We have a talk about being good.
It is good to be good.
It is bad to be bad.
We will all be good.
We sing a song about trees.
The bone in my bottom
cuts into the floorboards.
I'm not worried about the floorboards.
Miss reads out the notices
but nobody notices.
We stand up.
I pull my bottom bone
out of the floorboards.
We line up like soldiers,
like prisoners, like refugees.
We file out
in a sensible manner.
The hall is now empty.
Except for Jamie.

The Notices

Here are the notices:

It has come to my attention
that Dumpty, in the green class,
has been climbing the wall.
This is against school rules.
If he's not careful, he'll fall.

The same applies to the hill.
Get your water from the tap,
not the well.
It's a dangerous place.
Ask Jack. Ask Jill.

Food is not to be eaten in class.
This includes Christmas pie
in the corner; take note, Jack Horner.
The tuffet, as I have stressed,
is still out of bounds.

Speaking of food brings me
to school dinners.
If, like Jack Sprat, you are on
a special diet, please inform
Mrs Hubbard in the canteen.
Low-fat meals are now available.

Items of cutlery have been disappearing.
I want this to stop.
No more excuses like:
'I didn't steal that spoon –
the dish ran away with it.'
It just doesn't wash.

There will be a parents' evening
next Wednesday in the main hall.
The title of the lecture is 'Cat Rescue'
and the speaker will be Tommy Stout.
Music will be performed by
Little Boy Blue and the King Cole Fiddlers.

Finally, a word about dress.
The following items are not
part of the school uniform:
dusty skirts, rabbit skin,
trousers with knee buckles,
nightgowns. With this in mind,
would the following please stay behind:
Shaftoe, Flinders, Bunting, Winkie.

The Fun Times Table

One times fun is fun
Two funs are snigger
Three funs are a bit of a joke
Four funs are bigger
Five funs are chuckle
Six funs – guffaw
Seven funs are laugh out loud
Eight funs are roar
Nine funs are hysterical
Ten funs are over the top
Eleven funs are far too much
Twelve funs? Have to stop.

Bored

Tired of looking at teacher's writing.
Chalk bored.
Fed up with hearing about upcoming events.
Notice bored.
No interest in the white bits on the tops of waves.
Surf bored.
Can't stand flattening my sports kit to get rid
  of creases.
Ironing bored.

Can't be bothered to push plastic across squares.
Chess bored.
Don't want to see the Winter Olympics on TV.
Skate bored.
Prefer to sit down rather than dance.
Boogie bored.
Can't think of another verse for this poem.
Easily bored.

Questions, Questions

I'm always asking questions
But no one seems to know.
The sky, where does it end?
The wind, where does it go?

What keeps the stars from falling,
What holds the moon above?
Do dogs have dreams and nightmares,
Do rabbits fall in love?

Does time go on for ever,
And when did time begin?
Did God make all from nothing
And, if so, who made him?

I'm always asking questions
But no one seems to know.
Where do these puzzles come from?
Where do the answers go?

Classroom Love

I'm in love
with a girl in my class.
I won't tell you who
so please don't ask.

I like her smile.
I like her hair.
I feel good inside
when I know she's there.

Write a Poem About Anything

Write a poem about anything
My mind goes blank
No film in my projector
No fuel in my tank.

I look into the atmosphere
Doodle on a page
Write my name in capitals
Add my class and age.

The more I try to think of things
The less I think I think
My skull is overheating
My brain is on the blink.

Then these words come cranking out
Splutter, clink, clank:
'Write a poem about anything
My mind goes blank...'

Learn Everything You Can

Learn everything you can at school,
Take whatever you can get.
Then you can choose which bits to use,
And the rest you'll soon forget.

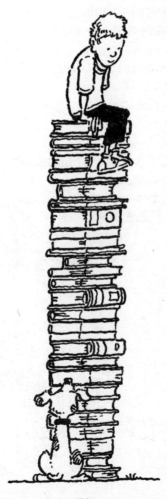

Ring-a-Ring o' Roses

Ring-a-ring o' roses
A pocket full of noses
Atishoo! Atishoo!
My trousers are all wet.

Starting School

My teacher's tall
The room is wide
The things I love
Are all outside.

My label's white
The class is blue
The ceiling's high
What shall I do?

The words are hard
My hand is sore
This sitting down
Begins to bore.

The day is long
The hours are slow
The noise is loud
When can I go?

William Wordsworth
*Bogey Poem**

My heart leaps up when I behold
A bogey in my nose.
As a child I felt that way
and still the feeling grows.
The pleasure has not withered –
It's better now I'm big.
Am I youthful, immature,
Or just a dirty pig?

* With apologies to William Wordsworth (1770–1850), who wrote a poem called 'My Heart Leaps Up When I Behold'.

School Dinners

The potato tastes like paper
The peas aren't even green
The slice of Argentinian beef
Is hidden by the bean.

The gravy's full of jelly lumps
The apple pie's gone wrong
But if I don't eat this dinner up
I won't grow big and strong.

If I Were Famous

If I were famous
I would never have to say who I am or
  what I do.
If I were famous
I could push my way to the front of any
  cinema queue.
If I were famous
Passers-by would stare at me and ask
  what all the fuss is.
If I were famous
You'd see my face on posters and the
  sides of London buses.

If I were famous
I'd have to wear shades so that no one
  could look into my eyes.
If I were famous
I could be silent and everyone would think
  that I was wise.
If I were famous
Everything I ever did would get recorded
  in the news.
If I were famous
My enemies would bow before me and
  polish up my shoes.

If I were famous
My teachers would stand in line and ask
  for my autograph.
If I were famous
My least funny jokes would make people
  crack up and laugh.
If I were famous
Everyone at school would want me to be
  their best friend.
If I were famous
I'd always worry that my fame was about
  to end.

Girls and Boys Come Out to Play

It's 1954. I'm small.
Girls do handstands against a wall
while boys have gangs which fight and spit.
You're in. You're on. You're out. You're it.

Young cowboys charge and drag their shoes.
They click their tongues to sound like hooves.
Their fingers point to fire a gun.
You're in. You're out. You're it. You're on.

The nurses stroke and feed their dolls.
Footballers score in net-less goals.
A conker splits; you lose or win.
You're on. You're out. You're it. You're in.

It's 1954. I'm small.
Girls in circles sneeze and fall.
A whistle blows. I hear a shout.
You're it. You're in. You're on. You're out.

Would You Do That at Home?

Would you stand on a chair at home, boy?
Would you slide along on the floor?
Do you jump down nine or ten stairs, boy?
Do you scrape your shoes on the door?

Do you slump like a slob at home, boy?
Do you pick your nose while you eat?
Would you stick your gum on a plate, boy?
Would you wipe your hands on your seat?

Do you act like a fool at home, boy?
Would you leave your room in a mess?
Do you chew like a cow in a field, boy?
As a matter of fact, sir, yes.

Innocence

The scratch, the rip,
The dash, the trip,
The punch, the splash,
The kick, the crash,
The knock, the bump,
The slide, the jump,
The push, the spit,
The cough, the hit.

The shout, the tear,
The smudge, the swear,
The shove, the prang,
The smash, the bang,
The trick, the slip,
The laugh, the quip,
The cheat, the fib,
The slur, the crib.

The cheek, the fight,
The nick, the spite,
The flick, the fling,
The slap, the ping,
The slop, the slurp,
The spill, the burp,
The miss, the mess,
The less than best.

I didn't mean it.

Stuck in the Middle of the Afternoon

It's just gone two and it's not yet three
It's way past lunch but it's not yet tea
It's not yet home but it will be soon
I'm stuck in the middle of the afternoon.

It's just gone sshh and it's not yet noise
It's way past books but it's not quite toys
It's bye bye sun but it's not yet moon
I'm stuck in the middle of the afternoon.

It's just gone work and it's not yet play
It's way past start but it still says stay
It's not yet go but it will be soon
I'm stuck in the middle of the afternoon.

Bees

Do bees have dreams
Do bees do wees
Do bees wake up
And stretch their knees?

Do bees read books
Do bees all see
Do bees have thoughts
Like you and me?

Do bees have maths
Or do P.E.
Do bees take tests
Like two plus three?

Do bees get As
Do bees get Bs
Do bees get cross
When bees get Cs?

Do bees buzz off
When bees get free
Do bees fly home
For bee-sized tea?

Do bees play games
Or see TV
Do bees have shows
on Bee Bee See?

Do bees flake out
Do bees like ease
Do bees lie down
To have some zzzzzeeeees?

Do bees make plans
Of where to be
Do bees like life
Or do bees just be?

School Bell

I love the sound
of the old school bell
(when doing a test
and not doing well).

Coming Home

Coming home, coming home,
coming home to the things I know,
to the clothes I wear,
to my favourite chair,
I'm coming on home to me.

Coming home, coming home,
coming home to the warm and safe,
to the big front door,
to the pet cat's paw,
I'm coming on home to me.

Coming home, coming home,
coming home to the space that's mine,
to the food that's fed,
to the unmade bed,
I'm coming on home to me.

Do Televisions Watch Too Many People?

Don't you think the telly gets bored
when it looks at you and at me
and says, 'Oh no, not them again
with their eyes on the old TV!
In this bit she sprawls on the floor,
then he gets a pizza and eats.
I know exactly what happens,
I'm fed up with all these repeats.'

Don't you think the telly gets tired
of the same old background of chairs,
of the same old windows and doors
and the same old quizzical stares?
It knows every line that we scream,
it's heard every insult before.
It sees all the drink that we spill
and the cheese that we tread on the floor.

Don't you think the telly gets mad
when we point and clamour and scream,
when we wave our fists in the air
and throw bits of food at the screen?
When tellies watch too many people,
it upsets the way that they think,
which is why the sound starts to fade
and the picture goes on the blink.

Can Hate Come Home?

Can Hate come home to play, mother,
For Hate is daring and fierce?
I'd rather you played with Love, my child,
For Love has a sister called Peace.

Can Pride come home to play, mother,
For Pride is clever and cool?
I'd rather you played with Humility,
For Pride can lead to a fall.

Can Lies come home to play, mother,
For Lies can duck and can dive?
I'd rather you played with Truth, my child,
For Truth has nothing to hide.

Can Greed come home to play, mother,
For Greed has so many toys?
I'd rather you played with Contentment,
For Contentment has far deeper joys.

Wish List

I wish I'd not listened at school
I wish I'd done all that was bad
I wish I'd not been so happy
And at least had a chance to be sad.

I wish I'd wasted more time
I wish I'd got less projects done
I wish I hadn't let homework
Interfere with my personal fun.

I wish I'd chewed far more pencils
I wish I'd flicked much more ink
I wish I hadn't been tempted
By teachers who said I should think.

I wish I'd counted more clouds
I wish I'd talked lots more rot
Then I wouldn't be lying here now
On the deck of my luxury yacht.

Think of All the Poor Children

I can't eat my burger
and Mum says,
'Think of all the poor children
starving in countries far away.'
And I think of them
with their dusty faces,
their large eyes
and their empty bowls,
I think of the white bones
of their cattle,
the rags of their mothers,
the screams of babies.
I think of the flies,
as hungry as the people,
sucking up tears and dirt,
but it doesn't make me hungry,
and my burger
with its blood-red sauce
and its ragged edge
cannot be sent by post.

Homework

I'll do my homework after tea
I'll do it at half-past eight
I'll do it at ten o'clock
I'll do it before it's too late.

I'll do it just before breakfast
I'll do it walking to school
I'll do it in the playground
(Whoops! I didn't do it at all.)

Eat it All Up

Crunch raw carrots
(see clearly in the dark)
Bite dog biscuits
(wag your tail and bark)
Feast on fishes
(purr loudly and miaow)
Grab loads of grass
(turn into a cow).

Swallow spinach
(get muscles like Popeye)
Suck up juicy sweat
(get dirty like a fly)
Wolf down a worm
(flap your wings and chirp)
Eat everything I've mentioned
(and burp).

Dancing in the Mirror

She was dancing in the mirror
with the music turned up loud
She was singing all the lyrics
and imagining the crowd
She was doing all the actions
with a hairbrush in her hand
She was smiling for the camera
and imagining the band.

She was dancing in the mirror
with the lighting turned down low
She was looking mean and moody
and imagining the show
She was spinning on the carpet
by her rumpled unmade bed
When her dad walked through the doorway
and her face turned cherry red.

Tall Poem

When I want to
know 'How tall?'
Dad stands me up
against a wall.
A book is laid
across my hair,
my back is straight,
my shoulders
square.

Thin lines are made
in pencil lead,
a tape is stretched
from heel to head.
Then up and up
the markings climb:
feet and inches,
name and time.

Lots of numbers
crowd the space
in between my
feet and face,
but up above
my highest height,
the wall remains
clean and white.

I wonder when
I'll be that high,
when things up there
will meet my eye.
Clean and white,
an empty page,
this wall awaits
my height and age.

— Mark 1/5/01
— Kate 8/2000
— Mark 5/2000
— Kate 4/2000
— Mark 1/2000
— Mark 8/1999
— Kate 2/99
— Kate 8/98
— Mark 12/97

For Harvey

When I was small,
   you were small;
a clockwork ball of fluff.
We rolled around
   on carpets;
your tongue was warm and rough.

When I was young,
   you were young;
a sprinting, barking blur.
We ran in parks
   and gardens;
I stroked your golden fur.

Now I'm still young,
   you've grown old;
your nose is flecked with grey.
Your wag has turned
   to wiggle;
your legs won't let you play.

When I am grown,
   you'll be gone;
you'll leave an empty space.
But in my dreams
   I'll hear your feet
and feel you lick my face.

Babysitter

Our babysitter called Flower
Was lazy, moody and sour
She sat in the chair
As if we weren't there
And charged £5.50 an hour.

A Life in the Day of the Sun

I remember the sun
as a baby – red and squashy,
cradled on the horizon.

As a child it danced with leaves
and looked at itself
in clear water.
We always knew that
it would be bright.

It did the usual teenage stuff:
throwing things (usually shadows)
climbing things (usually the sky)
becoming shy and hiding
behind clouds.

There was the day that
it burned someone's skin
and the time it set a forest on fire
but it said that it didn't mean to
and I believed it.

Middle-aged, it stuck
at the centre of the sky.
This was its peak.
It said it could go no higher.

As it got old
it became weaker.
Its energy seemed to be going.
At times it looked washed out,
pale.

The end came suddenly.
I think it must have been a shoot-out
or an ambush.
There was blood everywhere;
the sky was splattered.
Then everything went dark,
as dark as the grave.

Time for Bed

It's time for bed
Just two more minutes
It's time for bed
My game's not finished
It's time for bed
I feel afraid
It's time for bed
My bed's not made.

It's time for bed
Leave me alone
It's time for bed
I'm on the 'phone
It's time for bed
I feel too wired
It's time for bed
I'm just not tired.

It's time for bed
Can't I watch TV?
It's time for bed
Don't shout at me
It's time for bed
I need some toast
It's time for bed
I've seen a ghost.

Up the Wooden Hill

Up the wooden hill
Into sleepy land
Bathe in feather sea
Laze on cotton sand.

My Room

It's only a room.
But it's my room.
My space, my base,
my place in the world.

Brown bears stare
from a ledge up above.
I don't play with them now
but can't give them the shove.
They're stuffed
too full of love.

On the floor:
a pair and a half
of socks,
a bundle of keys
without locks,
a pair of goggles
in a box.

My life story
is neatly filed, piled,
pinned and hung:
passport photos,
posters, paperbacks,
pop stars, playing cards,
programmes and
pieces of paper.

It's only a room.
But it's my room.
Somewhere to go,
somewhere to sleep,
somewhere to be sent,
somewhere to hide,
somewhere to cry,
somewhere to dress,
somewhere to think.
Somewhere to be.

The Moon Has Got His Pants On

The moon has got his pants on,
he's dancing in the stars,
showing off his boxer shorts
to Jupiter and Mars.
He'd better get his trousers
and wrap up warm and tight
or he'll catch his death of cold
and we will have no light.

Water

You have no colour, no taste, no smell,
You fall, you run, you drip.
You come in rivers and lakes and seas,
We float, we swim, we dip.

You have no edges, no shape, no size,
You soak, you leak, you rain.
You come in trickles and mist and spray,
We pump, we dam, we drain.

You have no story, no age, no end,
You pour, you swirl, you slosh.
You come in buckets and sinks and baths,
We scrub, we rub, we wash.

Baths

I like baths.
They slow me down,
clean me up,
bring me round,
make me mellow,
turn me pink,
clear my head,
help me think.

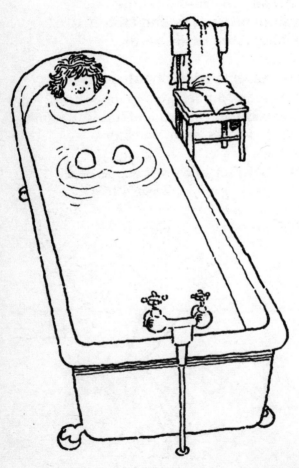

Washing

I'm washing off the blood
from playtime
I'm washing off the sweat from P.E.
I'm washing off the colours
from painting
I'm washing off the grease from my tea.

I'm washing off the pen
from English
I'm washing off the dust from the gym
I'm washing off the splashes
from puddles
I'm washing off today from my skin.

Nothing

What are you doing? Nothing.
And this time the answer is true.
I sit here doing nothing
because there is nothing to do.

I hold my head in my hands
I stare very hard into space
I swing my legs to and fro
and pick at a spot on my face.

How wonderful is nothing,
a subject that has no exam,
a time when, instead of 'I do',
I can simply say that 'I am'.

Prayer

Fell fast asleep
While saying a prayer.
When I woke up
Found God was still there.

A Book at Bedtime

I want a book at bedtime
I want a book in bed
I want to read a story
Or have a story read.

I want a big adventure
I want to see it all
I want to pull my knees up
And curl into a ball.

I want to feel some danger
I want to brave a storm
I want to have a duvet
That keeps me safe and warm.

I want to climb a mountain
I want to sail the deep
I want to hear a story
That sends me off to sleep.

I want a happy ending
I want a sudden twist
I want to hear you talking
I want a goodnight kiss.

The Eleven
O'Clock News

This is the eleven o'clock news.
I can't sleep.
I've counted the population of China
And all its sheep.
I've rolled over so many times
I'm almost dizzy.
I've told my brain to be quiet
But it's far too busy.

I can hear every creak and rattle,
Every hum,
The downstairs mumble of conversation,
Dad and Mum,
A cat on the roof of a garden shed
Down our street,
That river of blood inside my head going
Beat, beat, beat.

I try hard to think of nothing at all:
An empty cage,
A song that has no music and no words,
A blank page.
But into this huge space creeps a colour,
Comes a sound,
And sleep, like a stream, runs back to its home
Somewhere underground.

Night Clothes

Some people wear pyjamas;
they want to look the part.
Even when they're in their beds
they like to think they're smart.
With matching tops and trousers
they feel they are well dressed;
so if the doctor had to come,
he'd go away impressed.

Some people wear a tee shirt
that dangles to their knees;
something old and out of shape
that no one ever sees.
A present from an auntie,
a long unwanted prize,
a bargain from a basement
that didn't have their size.

Some people wear a tracksuit;
they think it keeps them fit.
They wake up in the morning
as if they've done their bit.
In their dreams they've jumped a lot
and scored some stunning goals;
they've run in the Olympic Games
and won their share of golds.

Some people wear a nightgown
like Willie Winkie wore,
made of something light and white
and hanging to the floor.
A matching cap of cotton
prevents the loss of heat,
while knitted boots with laces
bring comfort to their feet.

Some people wear pyjamas
but some don't wear a thing.
They sleep beneath the blanket
in nothing but their skin.
Some people say to do so
is really rather rude,
but underneath our nightwear
we all of us are nude.

Thank You

Thank you for the blanket
that spreads on my bed
Thank you for the pillow
that cradles my head
Thank you for the darkness
that rolls through the skies
Thank you for the tiredness
that closes my eyes.

Thank you for the windows
that keep out the storm
Thank you for the heating
that helps me stay warm
Thank you for the four walls
that make up my room
Thank you for the cold light
that falls from the moon.

Thank you for the loved ones
who sleep in this place
Thank you for the memories
that light up my face
Thank you for the silence
that comes with the night
Thank you for the feeling
that everything's right.